BE A PMP ACE IN 30 DAYS

How I aced the PMP exam in one attempt, without taking a break from work, and how you could do it too!

ROJI ABRAHAM, PMP

Be a PMP Ace in 30 Days

Copyright © 2017 by Roji Abraham

All rights reserved. No part of this publication may be reproduced, distributed, or transmitted in any form or by any means, including photocopying, recording, or other electronic or mechanical methods, without the prior written permission of the author, except in the case of brief quotations embodied in critical reviews and certain other non-commercial uses permitted by copyright law.

Paperback ISBN: 978-1519771896

CONTENTS

Introduction	1
About the PMP Exam	5
What stands between you and a PMP certification?	7
What you will get from this book	9
Required Study Accompaniments	12
The Weekly Study Plan	20
PMP Resource Websites	85
Jan 2016 PMP Exam Changes	88
Exam Day Tips	91
Interviews with Certified PMP Professionals	94
A Final Note	110
Your Feedback is Valuable	113
Join the Monthly Newsletter	115

INTRODUCTION

Congratulations on picking up a copy of this book!

You're in the right direction in your quest for PMP glory and before we start, here's my story.

I made a decision to pursue the PMP certification a year ago and subsequently obtained the mandatory pre-requisite of 35 professional development units (PDUs) towards the end of last year. Nevertheless, when I was looking for helpful material on the PMP examination online, to start my preparation, I was flooded with an overwhelming amount of information.

There were study guides and books of all kinds that included dozens of books claiming to be my ticket to PMP fame leaving me confused on what I should choose. I later realised that while some of these books online were useful, others were just misleading. For example, if somebody tells me today that anybody can become PMP certified with just two weeks of preparation, I would take that claim with a grain of salt because I know the actual number of hours that has to be put for preparation and to pass the exam – and it's far more than what a layman may assume.

Anyway, seeing all the scattered information I was rummaging through at that time, I realised I wasn't going to tame the PMP beast without a systematic process in place. After all, this is an exam that has a notorious fail percentage and several people I know failed the test (including some who failed more than once). Recently, a lady professional who attended PMP classroom sessions with me told me there were only four professionals from our class of over fifty, who actually attempted the exam and cleared it within the first 5 months.

Oops!

Given that the PMP Exam fee alone is US$405 (for PMI members) or US$555 (for non-members), failing at this exam isn't just de-motivating or a waste of many hours of time and effort, it is a costly affair too!

Eventually, I passed the exam on my first attempt and it took me less than 5 weeks from the time I got into the grind. I was graded 'Proficient' on four out of five sections and 'Moderately Proficient' on the last section. My success, nevertheless, was neither a fluke nor because of any outstanding brilliance of mine (which I do not claim to possess anyway).

I attribute my success to the clear plan I had defined and diligently followed taking into account my various constraints. I used a progressive learning technique by using easier guides and testing myself with basic questions first before moving to tougher guides and more grinding questions. I attempted simulation tests and did self-evaluations. I also marked weak areas and worked on them specifically. Lastly, I identified ways to link all the information I had learned and used various techniques to recall that information at will that helped me in the exam.

Sounds like a lot of work? Yes and no. Once you are motivated well enough, you wouldn't mind putting in the effort. Let me also add that I'm a man of limited means and the risk of losing a sizeable sum of money was very strong motivation for me to give it my all to emerge triumphant on my first attempt!

Following my success, I kept getting occasional calls from other PMP aspirants seeking advice and I came to realise that there were many others who could benefit from my learning. I understood that if I could recreate my journey in writing as accurately as possible it would be immensely beneficial to such people. That's how I came to write this book.

While there could be many roads one could take to reach the same goal, I can only speak for myself. I have 100% faith in the routine and the methods I followed and I'm sure that anybody who diligently follows the instructions I outline in this book will taste success.

Roji Abraham

November 2015

ABOUT THE PMP EXAM

Since you are already reading this book, it is unnecessary for me to give you a detailed introduction about the PMP exam. However, in the unlikely event that you are somebody with a limited idea about the PMP certification, let me give you a quick overview.

The Project Management Professional (PMP) certification is the most industry recognised project management certification in the world today for project managers and is offered by the Project Management Institute (PMI). There are a number of upsides to being a certified PMP professional, of which the following are the most well-known.

1. **A PMP certification gives you greater earning potential** – It is common knowledge in the corporate industry that PMP certified professionals earn well above the industry average for project managers and the Project Management Salary Survey (Eighth Edition) has mentioned that PMP

certified professionals earn, on an average 17% more than their non-certified peers.

2. **A PMP certification symbolises high quality** – The PMP certification is considered prestigious because it symbolises the certified professional speaks the global language of project management. The PMP examination measures a candidate's ability to apply knowledge in real situations and the ability to think critically. Therefore, it is implicit that a certified professional is capable of critical thinking and knows how to apply knowledge and methodology successfully while managing his/her projects.

3. **PMP professionals bring greater value to employers** – Professional studies have shown that when an organisation has more than a third of their project managers who are PMP certified, organisations complete projects more on time and within the estimated budget and scope. Therefore, organisations highly value PMP professionals and are more likely to choose such professionals over other professionals with comparable work experience but who are not certified.

There are many more advantages in holding a PMP certification, and to know more about the PMP exam and about the PMI, you can visit the official PMI website at http://pmi.org.

WHAT STANDS BETWEEN YOU AND THE PMP CERTIFICATION?

As an aspiring PMP candidate, you may have come across numerous books on the PMP examination including various voluminous study guides. You would have also attended class room sessions held by PMI's Registered Education Providers (REP) to procure the 35 professional development units (PDUs) which are a pre-requisite in order to apply for the examination.

But let me guess, you are not able to progress. Every time you pick up your study material you feel like you're falling into a bottomless pit.

Are these some of the problems stopping your from attempting the PMP exam?

1. You are simply not able to find time to prepare for the examination while working 9 hours a day and your office commitments or your boss stops you from taking leaves in order to prepare for the exam.

2. At times, you prepare at full steam for a week or so, and then some office work or personal commitment gets in the way. You lose momentum and can't get into the groove again.

3. You tried learning from the Project Management Book of Knowledge (PMBOK) and you are completely lost.

4. After studying for months, you are not sure if you will do well in the exam and don't know how to evaluate yourself before taking the leap.

If you face any or even all of the problems listed above, then this little book is exactly the thing for you.

WHAT YOU WILL GET FROM THIS BOOK

So before we go ahead and nosedive in to the content here, I really want you to have a clear understanding of what you will get from this book (and what you won't) so that nobody who reads this book has any wrong expectations from it.

Be a PMP Ace in 30 Days is my humble attempt at recreating the journey I undertook to become a PMP certified professional. This book captures the process I followed, the methods I used, the schedules I kept, and the way I honed my skills in solving problems that typically appear in the PMP exam. However, do note the following disclaimers:

1. <u>This book is not a one-stop study guide for the PMP exam</u>. You will need additional guides to prepare adequately for the exam and I will mention about these in the next chapter.

2. The 30 days mentioned is based on a calendar for people working 5 days a week with a prescribed

number of preparation hours as per the calendar I have outlined in later sections. You need to dedicate your time in line with the calendar schedule without slacking - this is not a schedule for lazy people!

3. You may have seen other books claiming that it is possible to get certified in fewer days, but from my experience, I believe that such programs will have a much greater risk factor and may cause you a burnout. The 30-day training period is optimum duration chosen based on my experience and discussions with various other certified professionals and trainers.

Did the above points sound a bit too rigid, making you sweat bucket loads already? Relax! This book is an easy-to-read guide and its instructions will be like an on-going conversation between the two of us. Here is my suggestion of how you should use this book for maximum benefit.

How to use this book

Read through the entire book once so that you have an idea of what is covered in this book. However, you need not go through the section titled The Weekly Study Plan in detail in your first reading.

Once you are ready to start your actual preparation, read the information provided in the aforementioned section at the beginning of each day for the 30-day period so that you have a daily target already set and you have an idea of what the key points for the day are.

REQUIRED STUDY ACCOMPANIMENTS

I have been giving suggestions about having a plan and a method to tackle the exam. So in this section, I am going to let you know how I got organised for starting my preparation. These are the various materials I had created or used. You need to get these ready before you start.

1. Study Guides

I used 3 different study guides and each of them served a different purpose. Don't get turned off because I said three instead of one. Trust me on this, you are better with these three and I am going to tell you the precise way I used them to get you the maximum result out of each guide.

A. Head First PMP

When you start preparing for the PMP exam, you will come across a lot of new terminology which you may not be that well-accustomed with during routine project management. However, the PMP examination tests you exhaustively (and not just what you know or you are accustomed t0). Therefore, it is essential that you get to ease your way in rather than stuff your brain with more information that you can withhold in one go.

I recommend using the Head First PMP guide by Jennifer Greene and Andrew Stellman because the book is great at introducing knowledge in a very informal writing style. It contains a lot of illustrations (never underestimate the power of visuals) and uses various analogies that can help you understand and recollect concepts easily. It is the best PMP guide for a beginner I have come across and I read it from cover to cover in the first 2 weeks of my preparation. However, the only drawback of this book is that it might not be enough to equip you to tackle some of the tougher questions in the exam.

You can buy this book from either your local bookstore or from Amazon.

B. PMP Exam Prep (by Rita Mulcahy)

Most PMPs swear by Rita Mulcahy's book. This guide covers each section in elaborate detail and is very articulate and coherent. Mostly importantly, the end of chapter questions in Rita's guide are the closest in structure and difficulty level to the actual questions asked in the PMP exam and I couldn't found any other question bank from any other website that was as useful as the ones covered in Rita's book. It is a must have.

Either borrow a copy of the book or buy it from Amazon; it is worth the price.

C. The Project Management Book of Knowledge (PMBOK)

This book is the official guide from the PMI and speaks the language of the PMI exam.

Here's a warning for those of you who just thought why not just get this and forget about the other two - the PMBOK is among the most boring textbooks I have come across.

While the PMBOK covers all the concepts and terms you need for the exam, it doesn't show how to apply these to solve actual problems. It seldom draws a parallel with real world examples or illustrates the mentioned concepts at work. It is simply a dry, fact-filled book and you have to toil to keep turning the page. If you know any friend who suffers from insomnia, make him lie on a bed and read fifteen pages of this book – rest assured, he will finally get that peaceful sleep that's always eluded him.

However, do not discard this book altogether because it is a useful resource to get free of cost if you have a PMI membership and most importantly, the PMBOK has process charts that are very valuable because they show visual representations of various inputs, tools and outputs for the individual processes. These visual representations, combined with the knowledge from other guides, help in understanding and remembering the individual processes much better. The PMBOK works well when coupled with the earlier-mentioned guides.

2. A Study Calendar

One of the first things I made before I started preparation was a study calendar. This is one of the most valuable resources I had because I still had regular office hours, my personal commitments, and couldn't afford to take a break from work.

The calendar helped me target timeslots that I could use (on working days especially) and helped me carve out time for a month in order to prepare for the PMP examination. The few points I made sure of while preparing my study calendar were:

The calendar didn't cause me to deviate from my regular weekday schedule by much and therefore my sleeping hours remained unchanged (sleep-deprived learning is counterproductive).

I squeezed out 4.5 hours for study on a weekday and 8 hours on weekends; not too much to cause a burnout but still quite demanding. Studying for 4-5 hours after work was initially a torture, but I once I got used to it, it was an elevating experience.

I used the first two weeks of study to go through the easiest guide (Head First) so that I could ease into the concepts before going through the more challenging guides and review questions later.

I kept a short 30 minute review at the beginning of almost every day and I also made sure I undertook simulation tests at strategic points in between, and ensured I worked on the weaker areas identified during these tests.

I have created a similar calendar for your use. You can download the study calendar in two formats:

a) Excel – If you want to modify the daily schedule time as per your need, download this format and then take a print for each of the weeks. The download link is given below:

http://bitly.com/pmpace-studyplan

b) PDF – This is not editable. You can simply download and print the calendar for use as it is. The download link is given below:

http://bitly.com/pmpace-studyplanpdf

3. The PMP Process Chart

The PMP process chart contains 47 processes that are divided into 10 knowledge areas and 5 process groups.

I strongly suggest that you take a printed copy of the process chart and stick it in a place where you always get to see it. I had my copy pasted on my cubicle wall in such a way I could see it whenever I turned my head. And within a few days I could recollect all the 47 processes without having to refer to my notes.

Now if you wondered whether you need to remember the names of all these 5 process groups, 10 knowledge areas and 47 processes, the answer is yes!

But here's something to cheer you up; I had remembered the process groups and the knowledge area names using mnemonics and it is fun. I will cover that in a later section.

I have also created a process chart that you can download and print for your use. You can get this PDF document by accessing the link given below:

http://bitly.com/pmpace-processchart

4. Stationery

Ah, we are back to basics here. Before you begin preparation make sure you have a notebook (the one made of paper and not the digital gizmo) and a pen or pencil in hand.

One thing that I learned was that we cannot easily retain an enormous amount of information by memorising it alone. Writing down key concepts and the necessary formulas for tackling the quantitative problems will go a long way in helping you retain the information effectively.

5. Digital Resources

While you don't need many digital resources to begin with, you will need to take periodic simulation tests eventually. And for this, you will need to access the internet. For the complete list of websites you will require, refer to the chapter PMP Resource Websites

I suggest attempting full length simulation tests and reaching a competency level where you can consistently score around the 75% mark. You can either attempt the free tests online, or purchase them from a reputed website.

Note regarding simulation tests: The PMI does not officially state what the pass percentage for the PMP exam is anymore, though previously it was set at 61%. However, the general consensus among the trainers and academics is that this is somewhere between 65-70% currently. Therefore, a person who can consistently score around 70-75% in simulation tests should pass the PMP exam too, in all probability.

All these resources put together should be sufficient to give you the necessary exam experience before the real PMP exam.

THE WEEKLY STUDY PLAN

In this section, I am going to break down the study plan into five weeks and show what needs to be covered each day during the entire period of study.

Hope you took a printout of the calendar I had provided in the previous section. This section will use that calendar for reference. In case you are going to modify this, do ensure that you still cover the suggested topics for the day in the same order as per the original schedule. Study for a constant number of hours on weekdays and extended hours on weekends and make this a routine.

Meanwhile, here are some tips to ensure that your work does not interfere with your study:

a) Inform your manager or team members beforehand that you will be preparing for the PMP in the weeks ahead and that you'll appreciate it if nobody schedules any calls or meetings after work hours since you are on a tight schedule.

b) If you have team members working under you, delegate any unavoidable after-office-hours work to your capable team members. Make sure you get their buy-in first, acknowledge their gesture and thank them for it.

c) If you have an option to work from home, now is the time to take it and save the time you spend on traveling to office every day.

Week One: First Iteration of Study - Getting Started

I started on a Saturday to have the whole day to myself uninterrupted by office work. Accordingly, my study week was from Saturday to Friday instead of the typical Monday to Sunday.

I also chose to start with the Head First PMP (HFP) guide as it is the easiest to read. Head First PMP also has a lot of fun exercises (crosswords, word match, tick the right box etc.) that you shouldn't skip. It helps in creating associations and remembering things easily, which is not possible by simply reading words.

Note: I used the 3rd Edition of HFP which covers the 5th Edition of the official Project Management Book of Knowledge (PMBOK) by PMI. Always use the latest edition so that you are up to date with any changes in the PMP exam.

The image provided on the next page shows the schedule (study) calendar for Week 1

	Schedule Calendar (Week 1)				
				Total Hours	**38.5**
	Day of Week	**Activity**	**Time slots**	**Notes**	**Hours**
Day 1	Saturday	HFP: Read through Introduction, Organisations, Constraints and Projects, PM Framework chapters (cumulatively 3 hrs) and Integration Management chapter (5 hrs)	9:30 am - 01:00 pm 4:00 pm - 6:30 pm 9:00 pm - 11:00 pm	Spend last 25 minutes on the Integration management review questions.	8
Day 2	Sunday	30 minute review of previous day's learning HFP: Scope Management Chapter	9:30 am - 01:00 pm 4:00 pm - 6:30 pm 9:00 pm - 11:00 pm	Have fun with the games in the chapter Spend last 30 minutes on the 26 review questions.	8
Day 3	Monday	30 min morning review. HFP: Time Management chapter	08:00am - 08:30am 07:00pm - 09.00pm 09:30pm - 11:30pm	Do excercies on float calculation, backward and forward pass	4.5
Day 4	Wednesday	30 min morning review. HFP: Time Management chapter	08:00am - 08:30am 07:00pm - 09.00pm 09:30pm - 11:30pm	Spend last 30 mins on 24 review questions	4.5
Day 5	Thursday	30 min morning review. HFP: Cost Management chapter	08:00am - 08:30am 07:00pm - 09.00pm 09:30pm - 11:30pm	Write down EVM formulas in your notebook for revision.	4.5
Day 6	Tuesday	30 min morning review. HFP: Cost Management chapter	08:00am - 08:30am 07:00pm - 09.00pm 09:30pm - 11:30pm	Spend last 45 mins on review questions (23 nos.)	4.5
Day 7	Friday	30 min morning review. HFP: Quality Management chapter	08:00am - 08:30am 07:00pm - 09.00pm 09:30pm - 11:30pm	Spend last 25 mins on review questions (20 nos.)	4.5

HFP - Head First PMP

Figure 1: Schedule Calendar - Week 1

Day 1 (Saturday) – Introduction, Process Frameworks and Integration Management

Start the day by reading through the introductory chapter and then the second chapter (Organizations, constraints, and projects). These chapters are a breeze and you wouldn't take more than an hour to run through them.

Once you are done with these, take a 5 minute break and then spend the next hour reading through the third chapter on **Process Frameworks.**

This chapter will talk about the 5 process groups and the 10 knowledge areas. There are 47 processes and each process belongs to one specific process group and one specific knowledge area. I had recommended taking a printout of the process chart and pasting it near your cubicle at work. Now let me make an additional suggestion: stick one copy of that process chart on the wall closest to your study table at home too. Anytime you feel like referring to a specific process, have a look at that chart.

For a beginner, remembering even the names of the process groups and the knowledge areas are a pain. Fear not, there is an old trick to remember these with the use of mnemonics. It's going to be fun.

The five process groups are **I**nitiation, **P**lanning, **E**xecution, **M**onitoring and Control, and **C**losure. Taking the first letter from each of the process group names, we can form a mnemonic that's easy to remember.

I Poured **E**mma **M**orning **C**offee

Now, don't sit and wonder who Emma is! Let's say she's a little girl who's going to help you remember a crucial bit of knowledge. Hope you won't forget that.

Likewise, there are also 10 knowledge areas you need to remember. They are **I**ntegration, **S**cope, **T**ime, **C**ost, **Q**uality, **H**uman Resources, **C**ommunication, **R**isk, **P**rocurement and **S**takeholder.

And here is the mnemonic I suggest you memorise: **I S**aw **T**win **C**ats **Q**uietly **H**aving **C**hicken **R**oast & **P**ork **S**andwiches.

Alternately, here's another one: **I S**aw **T**wo **C**ows **Q**uickly **H**aving **C**offee and **R**unning in **P**ink **S**tockings.

If you saw a really funny visual in your head, great! Do memorise and remember one of these two lines next time onwards. It'll help you remember the knowledge areas easily.

Once you have completed reading the chapter on process frameworks, use the rest of the day to read through the Integration Management chapter.

These are the various processes that come under the knowledge area Integration Management:

	Initiating	Planning	Execution	Monitoring & Controlling	Closure
Integration Management	1. Develop Project Charter	2. Develop Project Management Plan	3. Direct and Manage Project Work	4. Monitor & Control Project work 5. Perform Integrated Change Control	6. Close Project or Phase

Figure 2: Knowledge Area 1 - Integration Management

Start using your notebook, if you haven't already. Make a quick sketch of box figures for each of the 6 processes that come under the Integration process group.

When making your sketch, write down what are the inputs to each process and what are its outputs.

After you are done reading the entire chapter, spend 30 minutes to think and solve the review questions at the end of the chapter. After evaluating your answers, read all the explanations given for the answers. If you didn't understand something, refer back to the chapter.

If you got through this much on day 1, congratulations! Like the saying goes, "Well begun is half done." Get somebody to pat you on your back and get some good sleep.

Day 2 (Sunday) – Scope Management

Welcome to day 2.

Before you start reading the HFP guide's chapter on scope management, spend an hour and run through your notes from the previous day. We'll be using one hour today for review because you covered a lot of ground on the first day. Going forward, it will be just 30 minutes for reviews. Once you are done with the review, start reading the chapter on scope management.

Scope management is one of the most important process groups when it comes to the PMP exam because you can expect the maximum number of questions from this knowledge area. Scope, along with time and cost are called the **triple constraints of project management**. Essentially, these are what make or break a project. This is why understanding the scope management processes is vital to your success in the PMP.

Following are the various Scope Management processes grouped under the different process groups:

	Initiating	Planning	Execution	Monitoring & Controlling	Closure
Scope Management		1. Plan Scope Management 2. Collect Requirements 3. Define Scope 4. Create WBS		5. Validate Scope 6. Control Scope	

Figure 3 : Knowledge Area 2 - Scope Management

Key points to remember:

a) Draw the block figures in your notebook for each scope management process and map both inputs and outputs to each process.

b) Pay extra attention to the creation of **Work Breakdown Structure** (WBS) and how it is related to other processes in this group – this topic is an exam favourite.

c) Pace your reading such that you complete the first 3 processes before lunch.

Day 3 (Monday) – Time Management 1/2

Day 3 is when you will start feeling the pressure because it is the first weekday you will be using for preparation.

Start your day-3 with a 30 minute review of your previous day's notes. I used to do this always in the morning (as depicted in the study calendar).

Once you are back from work, split the 4-hour reading for the day into 2 parts – the first 2 hours should be before dinner and the rest two after dinner and before you head to bed.

I hope by now you have made a habit of scribbling notes into your notebook and drawing those little block diagrams for inputs and outputs for each individual process to be used for reference later.

Following are the various processes in Time Management:

	Initiating	Planning	Execution	Monitoring & Controlling	Closure
Time Management		1. Plan Schedule Management 2. Define Activities 3. Sequence Activities 4. Estimate Activity Resources 5. Estimate Activity Durations 6. Develop Schedule		7. Control Schedule	

Figure 4: Knowledge Area 3 - Time Management

The most important topic for today is **network diagrams**. Pay close attention to that section because it is connected to topics in the days ahead too. No review questions tonight!

Day 4 (Tuesday) – Time Management 2/2

This day's work will be a continuation of Time management and you will learn about some of the most important aspects of time management.

Key Points to Remember

a) Understand concepts like **float** and **critical path**; learn how they are calculated because these are regular (and easy) exam questions.

b) Do the exercises in calculating the **estimation techniques**. **Three-point estimate** is an exam favourite.

c) Do the exercises in calculating **Early Start**, **Early Finish**, **Late Start** and **Late Finish** using the forward pass and backward pass techniques. Once you get a hang of it, they are easy and will be questions you can certainly get right in the real exam.

d) Spend a little more time than usual in solving the review questions for Time management because these questions take more time that the qualitative questions you otherwise encounter. Focus on getting them right and do not focus on pace for now.

Day 5 and Day 6 (Wednesday, Thursday) – Cost Management

Cost management is the third of the triple constraints and many project managers think this would be the toughest topic to study because of the various formulas.

The truth couldn't be any further from this.

In reality, the cost management questions that come on the PMP exam are rather elementary. There are only about 6 formulas that you need to remember and any questions that come are just a variation of these.

The various processes that come under Cost Management are:

	Initiating	Planning	Execution	Monitoring & Controlling	Closure
Cost Management		1. Plan Cost Management 2. Estimate Costs 3. Determine Budget		4. Control Costs	

Figure 5 : Knowledge Area 4 - Cost Management

Key points to remember:

a) Write down the **Earned Value management** formulas in your notebook.

b) The most common questions related to this chapter test your knowledge of Cost Performance Index (**CPI**) and Schedule Performance Index (**SPI**) –

make sure you know that a CPI/SPI value **greater than 1 is a positive result** (you are within budget or within time) and **less than 1 is a negative result** (you are over budget if CPI<1 and behind schedule if SPI<1)

c) Like the time management questions, the cost management questions also need more time than regular qualitative questions. So when going through the review questions, take your time and solve them.

Day 7 (Friday) – Quality Management

The quality management chapter is one of the easier chapters you will be dealing with and questions from this chapter aren't usually confusing. From my experience, these questions are usually easy pickings. You should be able to comfortably cover the chapter in the scheduled 4 hours.

There are only 3 processes in this knowledge area; they are depicted below:

	Initiating	Planning	Execution	Monitoring & Controlling	Closure
Quality Management		1. Plan Quality Management	2. Perform Quality Assurance	3. Control Quality	

Figure 6: Knowledge Area 5 - Quality Management

Key points to remember:

a) The **seven basic tools of quality** is the most important concept you will be learning in this chapter

b) Familiarise yourself with terms like '**Rule of seven**', and the **80/20 rule** (Pareto charts) – these are exam favourites.

c) Don't get confused between the processes 'Control Quality' and 'Perform Quality Assurance' – this is a common problem for exam candidates.

Once you are done with the review questions, pat yourself on the back and smile. You have completed studying 60% of the exam syllabus in the first week! Good job!

Week Two: Getting into the grind

Hope you managed to keep up with the week 1 schedule. If you are a little behind schedule, you can use the first half of Day 8 to catch up on that. Here is your calendar for the week:

	Day of Week	Activity	Time slots	Notes	Hours
				Total Hours	**38.5**
Day 8	Saturday	HFP: Quality Management (any spillover from previous day) and revision HFP: Human Resource Management	9:30 am - 01:00 pm 4:00 pm - 6:30 pm 9:00 pm - 11:00 pm	Complete the 20 review questions	8
Day 9	Sunday	30 min morning review. HFP: Communications	9:30 am - 01:00 pm 4:00 pm - 6:30 pm 9:00 pm - 11:00 pm	Complete the 15 review questions	8
Day 10	Monday	30 min morning review. HFP: Risk Management	08:00am - 08:30am 07:00pm - 09.00pm 09:30pm - 11:30pm		4.5
Day 11	Tuesday	30 min morning review. HFP: Risk Management	08:00am - 08:30am 07:00pm - 09.00pm 09:30pm - 11:30pm	Complete the 20 review questions	4.5
Day 12	Wednesday	30 min morning review. HFP: Procurement Management	08:00am - 08:30am 07:00pm - 09.00pm 09:30pm - 11:30pm		4.5
Day 13	Thursday	30 min morning review. HFP: Procurement Management	08:00am - 08:30am 07:00pm - 09.00pm 09:30pm - 11:30pm	Complete 15 review questions	4.5
Day 14	Friday	30 min morning review. HFP: Stakeholder Management & Professional responsibility	08:00am - 08:30am 07:00pm - 09.00pm 09:30pm - 11:30pm	Complete 12 review questions on stakeholder mgmt and 10 on professional responsibility	4.5

Figure 7: Schedule Calendar - Week 2

Day 8 (Saturday) – Human Resource Management

Day 8 will be a relatively easy day because the first half of the day is for you to catch-up on the previous week's homework that spilled over and to do a revision of the previous section on Quality Management.

Human Resource Management is also one of the less stressful sections on the PMP exam and you should be able to comfortably complete it within half a day. There are four processes in this section across the five process groups as depicted below:

	Initiating	Planning	Execution	Monitoring & Controlling	Closure
Human Resources Management		1. Plan Human Resource Management	2. Acquire Project Team 3. Develop Project Team 4. Manage Project Team		

Figure 8 : Knowledge Area 6 - Human Resource Management

Key points to remember:

a) Focus on the leadership styles and motivation theories. You can expect a question on any one or two of the motivation theories such as **McGregor's Theory X and Theory Y** or **Herzberg's Motivation – Hygiene Theory.**

b) The four stages of team development (**Forming, Storming, Norming** and **Performing)** is also a topic from which you can expect a question or two.

c) The most important section in this chapter, from what I have seen, is the one on **conflict resolution techniques** – read through it carefully.

d) Are you still drawing the process blocks with the inputs and outputs? Do it for every process without fail.

Day 9 (Sunday) – Communications Management

Day 9 is yet another easy day. Hey, you're having a pretty stress-free weekend. Communications Management is a really short and sweet chapter. I remember covering both Human Resources and this chapter in one weekend with plenty of time to spare.

The various processes that are part of Communications Management are shown below:

	Initiating	Planning	Execution	Monitoring & Controlling	Closure
Communications Management		1. Plan Communications Management	2. Manage Communications	3. Control Communications	

Figure 9 : Knowledge Area 7 - Communications Management

Key points to remember:

a) Understand the four kinds of communication types – **Formal written, Informal written, Formal verbal** and **Informal verbal** and when each of them have to be used. Questions usually test whether you can identify the right communication type in a given situation.

b) Learn how to count the total number of **channels of communication** required for a team based on its size – the questions pertaining to this come in different forms and you are likely to get questions to calculate the total number of communication channels required for a given team size or a question on what is the increase in the number of communication channels when a team size grows from 'X' to 'Y'.

Day 10 and Day 11 (Monday, Tuesday) – Risk Management

Risk Management is a lengthy topic and hence, I scheduled two days to go through this. There are five processes split across two process groups. Refer to the table below:

	Initiating	Planning	Execution	Monitoring & Controlling	Closure
Risk Management		1. Plan Risk Management 2. Identify Risks 3. Perform Qualitative Risk Analysis 4. Perform Quantitative Risk Analysis 5. Plan Risk Responses		5. Control Risks	

Figure 10 : Knowledge Area 8 - Risk Management

Managing risks is a crucial part of project management irrespective of the size and scope of the project and therefore, you can expect a good number of questions from this topic (approximately 10% of all questions).

Key points to remember:

a) The sequence of processes here are like this as follows; identify the risks first, qualify them next and then quantify them. Once the risks are quantified, you decide how to act on them. **Always qualify before quantifying the risk.**

b) The various risk responses for negative risks (threats) are **Avoid**, **Mitigate**, **Transfer** and **Accept** while the responses for positive risks (opportunities) are **Exploit**, **Share**, **Enhance** and **Accept**. Commonly asked questions from this topic test whether you know which response to adopt in a given situation.

c) Pay attention to the various **information gathering techniques** to identify risks

d) The **Probability and Impact Matrix** (quantitative method) is an important method by which risk can be categorised into Low, Medium or High.

e) The **Expected Monetary Value** (EMV) analysis is an important tool for calculating which of any given set of risks is the most optimum to take. You may get a quantitative question on this section.

Day 12 and Day 13 (Wednesday, Thursday) – Procurement Management

I faced a handful of very tricky questions on procurement management when I attempted the PMP exam and for me this was one of the hardest areas to master despite having only 4 processes.

The 4 procurement management processes spread across the process groups as follows:

	Initiating	Planning	Execution	Monitoring & Controlling	Closure
Procurement Management		1. Plan Procurement	2. Conduct Procurements	3. Control Procurements	4. Close Procurements

Figure 11 : Knowledge Area 9 - Procurement Management

Key points to remember:

a) As part of the **Plan Procurement** process, you will often need to carry out a **Make or Buy Analysis**– in other words you have to make a decision based on what is most beneficial and cost effective for the company. Decision making using this analysis is the topic from this unit that has maximum probability to feature in a PMP exam.

b) The various types of contracts are a second important topic in this section. Know the various kinds of contracts such as **Fixed Price**, **Cost Reimbursable** and **Time and Materials.** Understand which type of contract is advantageous to the seller and which one is for the seller, which contract is of high risk to a seller and which contract is of high risk to a buyer.

c) Be acquainted with terms such as **force majeure** and **point of total assumption**

d) Have a good understanding of various procurement tools and techniques that are part of the Conduct Procurements process and when they are used.

e) Pay attention to various **proposal evaluation techniques**

Day 14 (Friday) – Stakeholder Management, Professional Responsibility

Welcome to day 14. Today you will be finishing the final process group and the section on professional responsibility.

There are 4 processes in Stakeholder Management spread across the process groups as depicted below:

	Initiating	Planning	Execution	Monitoring & Controlling	Closure
Stakeholder Management	1. Identify Stakeholders	2. Plan Stakeholder Management	3. Manage Stakeholder Engagement	4. Control Stakeholder Engagement	

Figure 12 : Knowledge Area 10 - Stakeholder Management

There is one little thing that you need to note here. If you consult the process chart, you will realise that of the forty seven different processes, there are only two which are part of the Initiating process group and one of those two is 'Identify Stakeholders' (The other is 'Develop Project Charter' from Integration Management). From known sources, the Initiating process group has 13% weightage in the exam and therefore, knowing just these two processes well could help you answer 22 out of the legitimate 175 questions (the remaining 25 questions are for evaluation purposes and not scored).

Key points to remember (Stakeholder Management):

a) A critical tool from this section is **stakeholder analysis.** The results from this analysis goes into the **stakeholder register;** you need to understand both and what are the types of analysis and what constitutes a stakeholder register.

b) Understand what a **Power/Interest Grid** is and what is the level of communication you need to maintain with a stakeholder based on his/her position on this grid.

c) Know the various **levels of engagement** for a stakeholder.

Professional Responsibility

Professional responsibility is a topic on the PMP that tests a project manager's knowledge and judgement on the Project Management Institute's code of ethics and professional conduct. While this topic has very little weightage (varying from 0- 2% maximum), you shouldn't get even a single wrong answer on this because these are easy pickings during the exam.

While you could answer most questions on this topic using good old common sense, I still suggest you go through this chapter once.

If you have reached so far, hurray! Do you realise you have actually completed all the topics for the PMP now? This is only the first iteration and you will need to go through all these topics again (the same way I did) with the next guide. However, now that you have your basics well in place, it will not be as difficult understanding them when going through the next guide.

We will start Week 3 with our first simulation test. I too had waited for 2 weeks before I took my first full length test and I did it after I reached this point in my preparation.

Week Three: Second Iteration of Study - Full Steam Ahead

During the third and fourth week, I stepped up the tempo. After having completed the entire Head First PMP guide and having attempted over 280 review questions from the guide, I was raring to go.

In the third week, I attempted my first simulation exam and it gave me an idea of where I stood. After the test, in which I had only a score of around 65%, I reviewed my incorrect answers and revised topics I scored poorly in and then started preparing with the more challenging PMP Exam Prep (PEP) guide by Rita Mulcahy and did a read-through of the corresponding knowledge area in the official PMBOK guide alongside. While there was much more to read in the same amount of time, it was easier because my foundation had been solidly built. At the end of each day, I spent time working out the questions for that knowledge area from the PEP guide.

The calendar for the week is given on the next page. I will be covering each of the days 15 to 21 after it.

	Schedule Calendar (Week 3)				
				Total Hours	**38.5**
	Day of Week	Activity	Time slots	Notes	Hours
Day 15	Saturday	Revision of Notes/Formulae from Day 1-14 Full Simulation Test #1	9:30 am - 12:30 pm 4:00 pm - 8:00 pm 9:00 pm - 10:00 pm	Simulation Test 1 (4hrs) Review ST-1 (1hr)	8
Day 16	Sunday	PEP: Project Management Framework and Integration Management PBOK : Integration management (quick read through)	9:30 am - 01:00 pm 4:00 pm - 6:30 pm 9:00 pm - 11:00 pm	Morning session: Complete questions on PM Framework and PM Processes Evening sessions: Complete the 43 questions on Integration Management	8
Day 17	Monday	PEP: Scope Management PMBOK: Scope Management (quick read through)	08:00am - 08:30am 07:00pm - 09.00pm 09:30pm - 11:30pm	Attempt 30 questions on scope management from PEP	4.5
Day 18	Tuesday	PEP: Time Management PMBOK: Time Management (quick read through	08:00am - 08:30am 07:00pm - 09.00pm 09:30pm - 11:30pm	Attempt 38 questions on Time management in PEP	4.5
Day 19	Wednesday	PEP: Cost Management PMBOK: Cost Management (quick read through)	08:00am - 08:30am 06:30pm - 09.00pm 09:30pm - 11:30pm		4.5
Day 20	Thursday	PEP: Quality Management PMBOK: Quality Management (quick read through)	08:00am - 08:30am 07:00pm - 09.00pm 09:30pm - 11:30pm	Attempt 31 questions on Quality from PEP	4.5
Day 21	Friday	PEP: Human Resource Management PMBOK: H.R Management (quick read through)	08:00am - 08:30am 07:00pm - 09.00pm 09:30pm - 11:30pm	Attempt 31 questions on HR Management from PEP	4.5

PEP - PMP Exam Prep
PMBOK - Project Management Book of Knowledge

Figure 13 : Schedule Calendar - Week 3

Day 15 (Saturday) – Revision and Simulation Test #1

The first half of today is reserved for revisions and to cover any spillover from the previous week. Run through the key areas in each of the chapters and check if you remember the formulas you learned (especially the Earned Value Management formulas) by writing them down. Also, test yourself by trying to draw entire table of processes and practice doing that within 5 minutes.

Hot tip: Every time before you attempt a simulation exam, spend a maximum of 10-12 minutes to draw the process table and to write down the various formulas. This is crucial to your success in the exam. It is easy to momentarily forget formulas after attempting so many questions under stress and writing these down helps you by not over-relying on your memory power. Doing this 'brain dump' is also allowed in the actual exam. However, since October 2016, it has been reported by many candidates that a brain-dump is now allowed only after the 4-hour exam timer starts. Therefore, you now need to practice doing a brain dump immediately after starting your 4-hour timer during simulation tests and then start attempting the 200 questions..

Attempt the simulation exam in the afternoon without getting distracted. If you are at home, tell your family not to disturb you for those 4 hours.

Many online simulators allow you to temporarily 'pause' the test and resume it later without the clock ticking away. Avoid doing this in your simulation test because you can't do this in the real exam and you need to replicate the exam scenario as much as possible in your simulation tests. If you need to take a toilet break, go ahead but with the clock ticking away still.

For your first simulation exam, I suggest one of the following:

The Head First practice exam on their website http://www.headfirstlabs.com/PMP/pmp_exam/v2/quiz.html

The practice test at the end of the Head First PMP guide (use this if only if the first option isn't feasible).

There are 200 questions to attempt in 4 hours and I suggest that you pace yourself to finish all the answers within 3.5 hours and use the last 30 minutes to review questions you had marked and skipped first time around. You will need to follow a similar technique in the actual exam.

After completing the test, take a break to refresh yourself and come back and review all the questions you got incorrect and the ones you had serious doubts on (even if you eventually got them right by chance). This way you will identify your weak areas.

Read the explanations provided for the answers and do go back and do a quick review of that section from the guide if you need to and then call it a day.

Day 16 (Sunday) –PM Framework, PM Processes and Integration Management

Today you will start the second iteration of preparation by using both Rita Mulcahy's PMP Exam Prep (PEP) and the official Project Management Book of Knowledge (PMBOK) side-by-side.

The general strategy I followed for the second round of preparation was to thoroughly read through PEP and then go through the corresponding knowledge area in the PMBOK. Since the PMBOK is rather dry, I used to quickly browse through the pages but keep my eye out for any terminology that I was not accustomed to read in detail.

Hot Tip: <u>The most important sections</u> from the PMPBOK guide were the overview diagrams at the beginning of each chapter and the data flow diagrams for each process. These are really useful for helping you understand and connect the various inputs, tools and techniques and the outputs for each process. Practice drawing each of them while going through each process.

Lastly, before reading the sections from the PEP, read your corresponding knowledge area notes you had taken down in your notebook in your first iteration of study (during the first two weeks).

On day 16, read the Project Management Framework and Project Management Processes chapters from PEP and then work out the problems at the end of each of the chapters in the first half of the day. In the afternoon session, read the Integration Management chapter from PEP thoroughly and then go through the same chapter in the PMBOK before attempting the end of chapter questions from PEP for Integration Management.

Key points to note (PM Framework and Project Management Processes):

a) Learn to distinguish between **Operations Management** and **Project Management.** Also learn to distinguish between a **project,** a **program** and a **portfolio.**

b) Learn the various types of organisations – **Functional, Matrix and Project-Based;** understand what is the amount of influence a project manager holds in each case

c) Understand what are Organisational Process Assets (**OPA**) and Enterprise Environment Factors (**EEF**); these are key inputs to most processes.

Key points to note (Integration Management):

a) Understand what a **Project Charter** is used for, who authorises it, what are the details captured inside it and what are the inputs to it.

b) Understand how a project is selected using economic models such as **present value (PV), net present value (NPV), internal rate of return (IRR), payback period** and **cost-benefit analysis** – one of the most common types of question in this section would be about choosing the best project out of many based on one or more of these criteria.

c) Understand the various types of depreciation – **Straight Line** and **Accelerated.**

d) Have a clear understanding of the Project **Statement of Work (SOW)** and the **Project Management Plan** (and its various constituents)

Day 17 (Monday) – Scope Management

On Day 17, save thirty minutes in the morning for a review of the previous day's notes and in the evening, read through the Scope Management process from Rita's PEP textbook (it should take you not more than 2 hours). Once that is done, quickly run through the corresponding chapter in the PMBOK in an hour. Scribble notes into your notebook when you come across key topics and keywords.

Use the last forty five minutes to attempt the thirty questions in the PEP guide and then review the explanations.

Key points to note from the day

a) Note down the inputs and outputs of each of the 6 scope management processes.

b) Learn what the various requirement gathering techniques are. There are frequent questions that refer to these indirectly. Among all techniques, these five are the most frequently referred techniques on the exam: **Facilitated workshops, Brainstorming, Nominal Group techniques, Affinity Diagrams and Delphi Technique**.

c) Understand the purpose of the **Requirements Management Plan** and the **Requirements Traceability Matrix.**

d) Note down what constitutes a **Scope Baseline**

e) Understand what a Work Breakdown Structure (**WBS**) is and how it can be broken down to **Work Breakdown Packages**. Learn how the WBS is linked to the **WBS Dictionary.** I consider the WBS the most important section in this knowledge area.

f) The **Validate Scope** Process relates closely with the **Control Quality process** – make sure you understand this relationship.

g) The **Control Scope** process, the last of the processes in this knowledge area, is where change control is often initiated – understand how.

Day 18 (Tuesday) – Time Management

Time management is the longest knowledge area with seven processes as you would be aware by now. This is also one of the sections from which maximum questions are asked during the PMP exam. You will need to stretch yourself today by an extra thirty minutes to one hour to ensure that you complete this chapter today.

Go through Rita's process chart to ensure that you know the right sequence of activities in time management starting from when you create the activity list.

Make sure you know how to draw a network diagram and sequence activities correctly by now (since you already had some experience in the first week). You may need to do them in the exam for several questions.

When you come across examples of network diagram illustrating how the **critical path** is determined and the **float** is calculated, do these yourself too side-by-side so that you are thorough with this.

Spend the last one hour attempting the 38 end-of-chapter questions.

Key points to note:

a) Understand terminologies like **rolling wave planning** and **decomposition** (also used in Scope Management to create WBP) - both are used in the **define activities** process

b) Know how to create network diagrams using **Precedence Diagramming Method** (PDM) and what the four logical relationships used to connect various activity nodes are.

c) Understand the concept of **lead** and **lag** time.

d) The various estimation techniques are an exam favourite – know how all of these very important techniques are used: **Analogous Estimation, Parametric Estimation, Three-Point Estimation** (also known as **PERT**) and **Triangular Estimation.**

e) Familiarise yourself with **Critical Path, Critical Chain, Schedule compression (Fast-tracking & Crashing), Resource Optimisation methods**

f) As stressed earlier, also be thorough in knowing how to calculate the **float** and **critical path** of any network diagram.

Day 19 (Wednesday) – Cost Management

Cost Management is without a doubt one of the most important aspects of project management and it is not surprising that it's one of the most important topics of the exam too.

You are unlikely to come across anything new in Rita's guide that you didn't cover earlier, but you will find some challenging questions among the end-of-chapter reviews. Cost Management questions involve basic calculation and hence typically take a bit more time to solve than questions from other sections that often need you to just think analytically and make a choice. But the advantage is that once you know the formulas you can always be sure of your answers since they involve only basic calculation.

Key points to note:

a) Know the various techniques used in the **Estimate Costs** process – most of these are actually the same as those used in time management such as Analogous, Parametric and 3-Point estimates. Additionally learn what **Bottom-Up Estimation** is.

b) Familiarise yourself with terms used in estimation such as **Reserve Analysis, Rough Order of Magnitude, Budget Estimate, Definitive Estimate** and **Cost of Quality.**

c) Revise the acronyms used in Earned value management (**PV, EV, AC, BAC, EAC, ETC and VAC**) and make sure you know how they relate to each other so that you can remember the formulas easily. There are only a few formulas and you need to write these down.

d) Remember that for both **Cost Performance Index** (CPI) and **Schedule Performance Index** (SPI), a value greater than 1 is good (within budget or on schedule) and a number less than 1 is bad (over budget or behind schedule) – questions on these indexes are almost a surety for the exam.

Day 20 (Thursday) – Quality Management

Before we start today, here is a question to see if you recollect your lessons from the Head First guide – what is quality?

In case you are still doubtful, **quality means the degree of adherence to requirements**. When the degree of adherence is very high, you call the product to be of high quality. You need to be able to distinguish between high quality and high grade as these are two different things altogether.

Quality management is one of the easier topics on the PMP exam and therefore, with a fair amount of effort, you should get all the quality-related questions right.

As usual, read through the PEP chapter on quality, brush through the PMBOK (focussing primarily on the charts) and attempt the end-of-chapter questions from Rita's PEP; there are 31 questions and you shouldn't take more than 30 minutes for these.

Key Points to note:

a) Learn to clearly distinguish between a **Perform Quality Control process** and **Control Quality process** – one implements **preventive action**, the second performs **corrective action.** You are likely to encounter questions that test your knowledge to distinguish the two.

b) Understand quality terminologies like **gold plating**, **marginal analysis** and **Cost of Quality**

c) Have a good grasp of **cost-benefit analysis**

d) You already know the **seven quality control tools**; make sure you're well versed in them by now.

e) Familiarise yourself with important techniques such as **Benchmarking**, **Statistical Sampling** and **Design-of-Experiments** (DOE)

Day 21 (Friday) – H.R Management

This is another relatively easy knowledge area, as you would have realised in your first iteration. The PEP guide, however, will provide you exposure to some more extensive details on the area. As we have been doing, read through the PEP chapter in detail, quickly run through the PMBOK (keep your eye out for any unfamiliar terms), and then attempt the end-of-chapter questions.

Key Points to note:

a) From the plan HR Management process, you need to know about the various charts, especially the **RACI matrix**

b) Understand the various **types of teams**

c) Familiarise yourself with terms like **Negotiation, Halo Effect, Virtual teams** and **Co-location**

d) Learn the **Tuckman Ladder** and 4 stages of team building – questions often give you a situation in the team and ask you to identify which stage a team is in.

e) The various **types of powers** of a project manager is very important – have an idea of when each power comes in handy.

f) The section on the five **conflict management techniques** is among the most important sections in this knowledge area – questions can be asked in which you need to identify which conflict management technique was used. Remember that **collaborating** (also known as problem-solving or confronting) is the most preferred and effective technique of the lot)

g) Make a note of the various work **motivation theories** (already covered in the first iteration

Week Four: Beginning Simulation Tests

As we move into week four, you should be ideally growing in confidence. Once the second iteration of study is complete, we will move our focus to the various simulation tests.

I did four simulation tests in week four and the results were much better than the first test I took. I'm outlining a similar model here.

Your schedule for the week can be found in the next page:

		Schedule Calendar (Week 4)			
				Total Hrs	**41**
	Day of Week	**Activity**	**Time slots**	**Notes**	**Hrs**
Day 22	Saturday	PEP: Communications Management PMBOK: Communications Management (quick read through) PEP: Risk Management PMBOK: Risk Management (quick read through)	9:30 am - 12:30 pm 4:00 pm - 8:00 pm 9:00 pm - 10:00 pm	Attempt 22 questions on Communication management Attempt 39 questions on Risk Management	8
Day 23	Sunday	PEP: Procurement Management PMBOK: Management (quick read through) PEP: Stakeholder Management PMBOK: Stakeholder Management (quick read through)	9:30 am - 01:00 pm 4:00 pm - 6:30 pm 9:00 pm - 11:00 pm	Attempt 37 questions on Procurement Management and 20 questions on Stakeholder Management	8
Day 24	Monday	Review notes Do 75 questions from Oliver Lehmann Do 50 PM framework questions from PMPDen	08:00am - 08:30am 06:30pm - 09.00pm 09:30pm - 11:30pm		5
Day 25	Tuesday	General review of previous day Simulation Test #2	6:00 pm - 7:00 pm 7:30 pm - 11:30 pm		5
Day 26	Wednesday	Review of Test #2 Simulation Test #3	6:00 pm - 7:00 pm 7:30 pm - 11:30 pm		5
Day 27	Thursday	Review of Test #3 Simulation Test #4	6:00 pm - 7:00 pm 7:30 pm - 11:30 pm		5
Day 28	Friday	Review of Test #4 Simulation Test #5	6:00 pm - 7:00 pm 7:30 pm - 11:30 pm		5

PEP - PMP Exam Prep
PMBOK - Project Management Book of Knowledge

Figure 14 : Schedule Calendar - Week 4

Day 22 (Saturday) – Communications Management & Risk Management

Given that today is a Saturday, you will need to cover two knowledge areas today. For communications management, use only the morning slot of three hours as this is the simpler topic of the two. Use the five hours post noon to study Risk Management.

Communications Management

Communications Management is an important topic because it is generally acknowledged that project managers spend up to **90 percentage** of their time communicating, in real project management.

If you recollect your lessons from the first iteration of study, you will remember there are three processes in communications management (spread across three process groups) – Plan Communications Management, Manage Communications and Control communications.

Read through the communications chapter of the PEP guide in detail, quickly scan the PMBOK for the same chapter, and finally attempt the 22 end-of-chapter questions in the PEP guide.

Key Points to note from this section:

a) Understand the four communication types (**Formal Written, Formal Verbal, Informal Written** and **Informal Verbal**) and in which contexts each of them are used – this has been already covered before in our first iteration

b) Understand terms like **effective listening** and the difference between **Interactive, Push** and **Pull** communication

c) Know how to calculate the number of **communication channels** required depending on the number of stakeholders – this was also covered before. Note that, by default, the project manager is always counted even if it is not explicitly stated.

Risk Management

This is a knowledge that can have some really tricky questions in the PMP exam. Can you recall all the processes in this knowledge area?

Read through the risk chapter of the PEP guide in detail, quickly scan the PMBOK for the same chapter, and finally spend the last hour attempting the 38 end-of-chapter questions in the PEP guide and reviewing your answers.

Key Points to note from this section:

a) Review the various information gathering methods for identifying risks; also understand other analysis methods like **SWOT, checklist analysis, Assumptions analysis** and **Diagramming Techniques** (e.g.: Ishikawa method)

b) The inputs and outputs of the **Perform Qualitative Risk Analysis** and the **Perform Quantitative Risk Analysis** are important.

c) Learn what information is captured in a **Risk Register**

d) Have a good understanding of **Probability and Impact Analysis** and the **Expected Monetary value Analysis** – you can expect some simple problems related to either or both.

e) **Decision Tree Analysis** is very important.

f) Have a thorough understanding of **Risk Response Strategies** for both **Threats** (negative risks) and **Opportunities** (positive risks)

Day 23 (Sunday) – Procurement Management & Stakeholder Management

With today's topics, we will be completing our second iteration of study.

Use the first five hours of today's schedule for Procurement Management Study and the last three hours of the schedule for Stakeholder management (this is the easier of the two topics). Spend the first 10 minutes to revise the previous day's notes.

Follow the same pattern of reading through Rita's PEP first, followed by the quick read through of the PMBOK (paying attention to process charts) and then finally attempt the end-of-chapter questions. Do the exercise in each of the two knowledge areas.

Key points to Note (Procurement Management):

a) The Procurement Statement of Work **(SOW)** is one of the most crucial documents from the procurement process and therefore you need to have a thorough understanding of its constituents and its purpose. Other important documents are Request for Proposal **(RFP)**, Invitation For Bid **(IFB)** and Request for Quotation **(RFQ)** – make a note of when these documents are used and what they are used for.

b) Procurement always involves a buyer and a seller. Note that PMP questions are always from a buyer's point of view unless stated otherwise.

c) **Make-or-Buy analysis** related questions are among the most common questions you'll find on this section in the PMP exam– have a good idea on how to do such analysis.

d) **Types of Contracts** (Fixed, Cost-reimbursable & Time and materials), as stated earlier in this book, are extremely important and will be tested comprehensively in the PMP exam.

e) Practice problems that involve the **Point of Total Assumption** and Incentive calculations

f) Familiarise yourself with terms like **Prequalified Seller List, Bidder Conferences,** and **Claims Administration**. While there are many more, these are some that are frequently referred to in the exam.

The PMP Exam Prep guide doesn't bring much new knowledge on the Stakeholder management process and you would have learned most of this during the first iteration using the Head First guide. Nevertheless, I'm still marking the key sections here. Attempt the end-of-chapter questions after reading this section and skim through the same chapter in the PMBOK.

Key points to Note (Stakeholder Management):

a) The **Identify Stakeholder process** is the only other process, apart from Develop Project Charter, in the Initiating process group. The first thing a project manager has to do after being assigned to a project is identify stakeholders and create a **stakeholder register** –this section is an exam favourite and questions from this section are usually easy pickings on the exam.

b) Understand what approach to adopt with specific stakeholders based on their position on the **Power/Interest Grid** –you can see an example of this in the PMBOK

c) Have an understanding of the various **engagement levels** of stakeholders – this is illustrated in the PMBOK.

Day 24 (Monday) - Revision

Now that you have completed two full iterations and also skimmed the PMBOK, you should be thorough with all the concepts across all knowledge areas. Today will be a less hectic day. However, instead of sitting idle, practice the following:

1. Go through your notes across the two iterations. If you feel there is any topic that you can't remember, try reading it again from Rita's PEP or even the PMBOK.

2. Practice drawing the process chart with all the 47 processes from memory.

3. Practice writing down all the various formulas, one knowledge area at a time, that you will need for the exam.

4. Spend 75 minutes in attempting the 75 free questions on **Oliver Lehmann's website** and then review all your answers (both the wrong ones and the ones that you got right by chance). These questions are quite challenging but provide valuable learning. Website details are provided in the chapter 'PMP Resource Websites'.

5. Spend 50 minutes in attempting the 50 free questions related to the Project management Framework from the PMP Den website. Website

details are provided in the chapter 'PMP Resource Websites'.

Day 25 (Tuesday) – Simulation Test #2

Today you'll be taking your second full length simulation test. Make sure that you are free from all distractions for the entire four hour duration of the simulation test. Spend thirty minutes to one hour revising formulas, and then attempt the exam in one go. Use 12 minutes before the commencement of the exam to write down the various formulas and to draw process chart from memory. Practice this in every simulation test.

Tip: Always time yourself to answer questions at the rate of one question per minute on an average. This means that you will practice to go through all the 200 questions in 3 hours and 20 minutes. This gives you the last 40 minutes to attempt questions you had tagged for review.

If you haven't purchased any simulation tests from any website, use the free test from the PM Study website this time. Website details for this website are provided in the chapter 'PMP Resource Websites'.

The first few times you will feel drained after the exam, so just call it a day after the test and review the exam the next day.

Day 26 (Wednesday) –Simulation Test #3

Spend the first hour of today going through your wrong answers and the answers you had doubts on during the previous day's simulation test #2.

Tip: When reviewing the previous day's test, you will come across some terms/topics or keywords you aren't familiar with (or forgot). Write down these key terms in your notebook so that you can check them again.

Take a short break, have a light dinner and then sit for the next four hours attempting your third simulation test.

If you are still looking forward to practice using free tests, use the Exam Central website this time. Website details are provided in the chapter 'PMP Resource Websites'. There are an unlimited number of free tests here, so you can use the same link for the remaining simulation tests too.

Day 27 (Thursday) –Simulation Test #4

Follow the same routine from the previous day. Review questions from the previous day's test, write down noticed problem areas, check them and then go ahead and attempt the next simulation test.

When revising problem areas, I suggest checking Rita's PEP or the PMBOK. This is because these guides are more comprehensive than the Head First guide (which was more suited for a beginner).

Day 28 (Friday) –Simulation Test #5

Follow the same routine from the previous day. Review questions, write down noticed problem areas, check them and then go ahead and attempt the next simulation test.

Note: There is a full length simulation test at the end of Rita Mulcahy's PEP guide. If you haven't done this yet, I strongly suggest you attempt this – it has excellent questions. But, if you want to skip this now, go through these questions on the last day instead of an online simulation test #7

Week Five: Fine Tuning and Final Simulation Tests

There are only 2 days remaining from our 30 days, and in these last two days, we will iron out the final problem areas before attempting a couple more tests and be fully ready for the actual PMP Exam.

	Day of Week	Activity	Time slots	Notes	Hrs
		Schedule Calendar (Week 5)		**Total Hours**	**16**
Day 29	Saturday	Review SIM Test #5 and fine-tune problem areas. SIM Test #6 & review	9:30 am - 12:30 pm 4:30 pm - 8:30 pm 9:30 pm - 10:30 pm	Attempt sample questions knowledge area-wise if required.	8
Day 30	Sunday	SIM Test #7 (optional) General review	9:30 am - 12:30 pm 4:30 pm - 8:30 pm 9:30 pm - 10:30 pm	If not attempting Test #7, go through the 200 full length test questions from Rita's PEP.	8

Figure 15 : Schedule Calendar - Week 5

Day 29 (Saturday) – Fine-Tuning & Simulation Test #6

Once you are done reviewing Simulation test #5, check the following:

1. Are you able hit around the 70-75% mark or more in the past 2-3 tests?

If you are, then you are doing quite well. Congratulations! You are almost ready for the big day. If you are not, you'll find the remaining information below helpful before you progress to the remaining simulation tests.

2. Are you running out of time on the exam?

If you are, you need to certainly sort this problem out. Ideally, you need to finish attempting all 200 questions within three and half hours maximum. If you are not, these are the typical reasons you run out of time:

i) You spend too much time on tricky questions and lose track of time

ii) You can't recollect formulas or process names at times and spend time thinking about them before being able to answer

These are the approaches that I took to address these problems when I encountered them during simulation exams.

For the first issue, I made a mental note to just mark a question for review, guess the most likely answer and move on to the next question if I was not anywhere in sight of a definitive answer at the end of sixty seconds. The penalty for running out of time is far more than what you could gain by solving a handful of tricky questions at the risk of getting timed out. If you mark such questions and move on quickly enough, you'll even get time at the end to come back and spend more time on such question.

For the second issue, there's one helpful solution: practice drawing the process chart and writing down the formulas at the beginning. It is a tremendous strain on your mind to instantly recall formulas and process names under stress and it is far easier to refer to what you wrote on paper.

2. Are you consistently getting answers wrong on a specific knowledge area?

I had encountered this problem with Procurement Management. For this, do one more reading of the PMBOK/PEP and then read through the questions in Rita's PEP guide.

Try out some free questions on your weaker topic with online resources. You can try the Prepare PM website (link is provided in the next section) which will allow you to test your knowledge on a specific knowledge area

Once you feel confident that you have sorted out your knowledge gaps, go ahead and attempt your next simulation exam #6. Finish the review the same day since you will have enough time for it.

Day 30 (Sunday) –Optional Simulation Test #7 and Review

Today, you will be attempting your last simulation test and you should feel extremely confident by now if you have followed the instructions in this book judiciously.

If were already touching the 70- 75% mark in the last 2 or 3 simulation tests, you can actually skip this test and just practice questions at leisure. Also, if you haven't done the 200 questions at the end of Rita Mulcahy's PEP guide yet, do it today.

However, don't attempt any simulation tests one day before the exam. You need to get ample rest for your mind and body. Spend the last day before exams just reading through your notes and practice drawing the process chart.

PMP RESOURCE WEBSITES

Here are some useful websites (I had referred to some of these earlier in this book too) where you will find good quality practice questions (including free ones) for the PMP exam.

1. **Head First Labs** – This is the website of the makers of the Head First guide. You can attempt a free simulation exam here. The website link is given below:

http://www.headfirstlabs.com/PMP/pmp_exam/v2/quiz.html

2. **Oliver Lehman** – This is a very popular website with many resources for the PMP. You can also try out the 75 free questions here. The website link is given below:

http://www.oliverlehmann.com/pmp-self-test/75-free-questions.htm

3. **PMStudy.com** – I found it useful because it provides a timed full length simulation test for free. You also have an option to purchase a pack of 4 tests for a cost of $60. The website link is given below:

http://www.pmstudy.com/enroll.asp#PMP

4. **PMP Den** – At the time I was preparing for PMP, they had provided free questions for each section and these questions were of high quality. But right now, you have to pay $12 to have access to over 1400 questions (which is a fair price). You can also attempt free questions on the PM Framework here. The website link is given below:

http://www.pmpden.com/pmbok-5-exam-questions/

5. **Exam Central** - This is not a PMP-focussed website, but they provide an unlimited number of free tests for the PMP which you will find so handy in your preparation. The website link is given below:

http://www.examcentral.net/pmp/pmp-exam-questions

6. **Free PM Exam Simulator** – This website provides you with 170 free PMP questions on registration (not-charged). The website link is given below:

http://free.pm-exam-simulator.com/

7. **Prepare PM** – This website is useful because it provides questions sorted by knowledge area and comes in handy when you want to brush up a specific knowledge area. The website link is given below:

http://preparepm.com/pmp/questions.html

8. **PMZilla** – This website lists a comprehensive number of PMP exam resources from other websites in one location. The website link is given below:

http://pmzilla.com/free-pmp-exam-mock-questions-important-links-best

JANUARY 2016 PMP EXAM CHANGES

While there has been a lot of furore over the new changes in the PMP exam effective from January 2016, the reality is that these changes are very minimal in nature and the exam still continues to use the Fifth Edition of the PMBOK, as it used to before these new changes. However, for the record, the noticeable changes were five new tasks added across the various process groups:

1. **Initiating Process Group Changes** – This group has three new tasks and they are described below:

a) Identify key deliverables based on the business requirements, in order to manage customer expectations and direct the achievement of project goals.

b) Conduct benefit analysis with stakeholders (including sponsor, customer, subject matter experts), in order to validate project alignment with organizational strategy and expected business value.

c) Inform stakeholders of the approved project charter, in order to ensure common understanding of the key deliverables, milestones, and their roles and responsibilities.

2. **Planning Process Group Changes**– This group has one new task:

a) Develop the stakeholder management plan by analysing needs, interests, and potential impact, in order to effectively manage stakeholders' expectations and engage them in project decisions.

3. **Executing Process Group Changes**– Two new tasks added in this group

a) Manage the flow of information by following the communications plan, in order to keep stakeholders engaged and informed.

b) Maintain stakeholder relationships by following the stakeholder management plan, in order to receive continued support and manage expectations.

4. **Monitoring & Controlling Process Group Changes**– Over here two new tasks were added:

a) Capture, analyse, and manage lessons learned using lessons learned management techniques, in order to enable continuous improvement.

b) Monitor procurement activities according to the procurement plan, in order to verify compliance with project objectives.

Note: There were no new tasks added to the Closing Process Group

The general consensus is that these changes are just slight improvements over the existing exam and their effects won't really make or break a PMP exam candidate's chances. A candidate just needs to be aware of them.

As a last word on this topic, since the general focus of these changes is around stakeholder concerns, it might just be prudent to focus a bit more on Stakeholder Management related topics on the exam than before.

EXAM DAY TIPS

While you will find abundant information about what you should do and what you shouldn't on the exam day, I thought I'd write down information that I found the most useful.

1. Ensure that you prepare to reach the exam centre at least an hour before your appointment schedule and start from home accordingly. This ensures that you don't stress yourself out in case of unforeseen circumstances such as excessive traffic or you taking more time than expected to locate the testing centre.

2. Do not have a heavy meal before the exam and take a snack and a drink with you that you can consume during the break.

3. Before the exam commences, you will be given a booklet and two pencils. You will be provided a 15-minute interval before the exam commences to read instructions, but you can complete this within a few minutes. Earlier, students used to utilise this bonus

time for creating a brain-dump of the various formulas and the process chart using the pencil and booklets. However, the rules have changed now and a student can do a brain-dump only after the exam timer starts. Nevertheless, when under stress, your brain-dump will turn out to be extremely useful. Practice this during your mock tests also, as advised in an earlier section of this book

4. Keep a target of completing a fixed number of questions in a given duration of time. I strongly suggest keeping a target of attempting 1 question per minute in your first pass. Here's a sample breakdown you could follow for pacing your exam:

Do a brain-dump	10 minutes
Complete 75 questions	1 hour 25 minutes
Complete 150 questions	2 hours 40 minutes
Take a 5 minute break	2 hours 45 minutes
Complete 200 questions	3 hours 35 minutes
25 minute review of marked questions	4 hours

5. If you cannot reach a clear answer after reading a question, select the most likely answer or even a random answer (there are no negative marks) and then mark that question for review before moving on. Do not waste time pondering over any single question. In the worst case scenario using this approach, even if you don't get time to come back to this question, you still have a 25% probability of getting the answer right because of chance.

6. Do your best to complete all 200 questions in three and half hours or less to leave you at least thirty minutes to spend on the questions you marked for review. Follow this approach even when taking your simulation tests.

INTERVIEWS WITH CERTIFIED PMP PROFESSIONALS

I have experienced myself that the best advice I received before attempting the PMP examination came from professionals who went through the PMP journey successfully themselves too. Therefore, I got in touch with a few successful PMP professionals from around the globe and interviewed them with carefully crafted questions to get their first-hand perspectives.

In the five interviews below, each professional will give their perspectives on how the PMP helped them, what their biggest obstacles were while preparing for the exam, how they overcame these obstacles, useful exam strategies, and what their most important advice for cracking the exam is.

You will find these interviews immensely useful and encouraging.

Interview #1 with PMP Professional Rahul Mysore

PMP Number: 1696451

Brief profile: Rahul is a Senior Project Manager driving transformational initiatives in Canada's largest bank to improve client satisfaction, reduce operational costs and contribute to increase in bank's bottom line.

1. How has the PMP certification helped you in your career?

In the short term, the PMP has helped me greatly. The PMP certification has become the entry criteria for senior PM roles. In the medium to long term, armed with the PMP, I hope to break the glass ceiling into Sr. Leadership roles.

2. What was the biggest obstacle you faced in preparing for the PMP and how did you overcome it?

One of the biggest obstacles was the time I could spare for preparation while balancing a stressful and busy day job and my responsibilities at home with my family in the evening. This also made me postpone my PMP preparation continuously.

I consciously decided to break the vicious cycle by enrolling into a weekend crash course to prepare and write the exam soon after when learning was still fresh in mind.

3. What are the 3 most important resources that helped you prepare for the exam?

a) The weekend all-day crash course

b) Simulation tests

c) Flash cards

4. What are the 3 most useful strategies you employed to crack the PMP exam?

a) Application of knowledge areas as prescribed by the PMBOK

b) Unlearning industry practices and embracing PMBOK best practices

c) Time management

5. What would your most important advice to any PMP aspirant who wants to crack the exam on the first attempt be?

While a good understanding of best practices as prescribed by the PMBOK is a good foundation, focus on applying the foundation to scenarios to help you tackle questions better in the exam.

Interview #2 with PMP Professional Wan-Yu Chen

PMP Number: 472988

Brief profile: Wan is a professional from Taiwan. She is an advanced specialist in the program control division of a telecommunications organisation.

1. How has the PMP certification helped you in your career?

The PMP course helped me learn good concepts in project management and also helped me build good network connections that have been valuable.

The PMP certification has also helped me get many opportunities to carry out some projects in different fields and also support a consultancy company to perform challenging projects.

2. What was the biggest obstacle you faced in preparing for the PMP and how did you overcome it?

I got only limited time for PMP preparation since I was occupied with my job during the day time. Therefore, I set a clear target day to attempt the exam and get certified and accordingly, created a day-by-day plan and forced myself to finish learning in time for the exam.

3. What are the 3 most important resources that helped you prepare for the exam?

a) PMBOK

b) PMP lectures

c) Online test resources such as simulation tests for the PMP

4. What are the 3 most useful strategies you employed to crack the PMP exam?

a) Maintain a steady pace when attempting questions

b) Identify the main topic from the question at first and then read the detail

c) Double check answers

5. What would your most important advice to any PMP aspirant who wants to crack the exam on the first attempt be?

Read the study materials systematically, try to understand the content based on work experiences, always use simulation exams to identify your blind points and train yourself to answer at the right pace.

Interview #3 with PMP Professional

Sanjeev Sharma

PMP Number: 1702471

Brief profile: Sanjeev is based in India and is a Project Manager with a leading Indian IT multinational having over 14 years of experience, mainly in program and project management.

1. How has the PMP certification helped you in your career?

Having a PMP credential on my resume did help me in getting shortlisted for the openings internally within the organization. Having a PMP certification is a feather in your cap. It formally declares your experience and skills in the domain of project management and separates your CV from the pack.

2. What were the biggest obstacles you faced in preparing for the PMP and how did you overcome it?

a) Lack of sample practice questions in line with actual PMP exam format (there are many available on internet but they don't give the exact feel of real questions).

b) Taking the time out of my schedule to dedicatedly prepare every day (had lost touch of studies).

c) Pressure of finishing all questions in time and also the difficulty in sitting for an extended period of four hours.

3. What are the 3 most important resources that helped you prepare for the exam?

a) Sample questions grouped on knowledge-area in the PMP website (one needs PMI membership to access this part of the website)

b) PMBOK by PMI

c) Head First PMP by O'Reilly Media

4. What are the 3 most useful strategies you employed to crack the PMP exam?

a) Memorizing the process diagram and the formulas.

b) Elimination method (removing the obvious NOs from the answer choices).

c) Time management - Not wasting much time on questions in which there was no clear answer even after eliminating the obviously wrong answers (and attempting them in the end).

5. What would your most important advice to any PMP aspirant who wants to crack the exam on the first attempt be?

a) Process chart should be learnt by heart

b) Try as many complete sample questions including complete time-bound sample exams (4-5 complete exams should be enough).

c) Keep minimal gap between the classroom training and the exam (not more than 3 months).

Interview #4 with PMP Professional

Ankur Gupta

PMP Number: 1492242

Brief profile: Ankur has been a seasoned project management and customer engagement professional for over 10 years, and has managed global client portfolios across continents for project & service delivery and pre-sales functions.

1. How has the PMP certification helped you in your career?

It has made me more recognised within and outside my organization. It has also helped me in having a better understanding of project management and has helped me practice leading my respective projects with more confidence and greater consistency in delivery.

2. What were the biggest obstacles you faced in preparing for the PMP and how did you overcome it?

a) Translating PMBOK information into exam usable information for the questions that appear in the exam.

b) There were limited mock test options to simulate the exam experience and test my readiness for the exam in advance.

3. What are the 3 most important resources that helped you prepare for the exam?

a) PMBOK

b) The 5-day classroom training by a PMI REP (Registered Education Provider).

c) Rita Mulcahy's guide (for exam preparation).

4. What are the 3 most useful strategies you employed to crack the PMP exam?

a) Focussed on different knowledge areas based on their weightage.

b) Didn't skip any knowledge area and ensured minimal understanding of each.

c) I wrote down all formulas from memory on the given plain sheet inside the exam room as soon as I was seated and allocated the paper and pencil.

5. What would your most important advice to any PMP aspirant who wants to crack the exam on the first attempt be?

Do not be bothered by the jargon and try to learn and understand the concepts, and try to visualize how the concepts apply at work. The PMP is just another exam. If you have reached PMP exam, you must have already passed many other exams in life. The PMP is nothing out of the world. Don't worry.

Interview #5 with PMP Professional

Harsha Arunachala

PMP Number: 1713021

Brief profile: Harsha lives in Johannesburg, South Africa, and is a Regional Practice Manager in a global multi-national Information Technology company. In a career spanning 10 years, he has worked in various pre-sales, professional services and customer management roles and has catered to a wide array of global clients.

1. How has the PMP certification helped you in your career?

The PMP certification has equipped me with the knowledge of concepts to carry out project management effectively and has more importantly empowered me with the ability to "measure" progress and end goals in an otherwise subjective practice.

2. What were the biggest obstacles you faced in preparing for the PMP and how did you overcome it?

The biggest obstacle I faced was time management. It was quite challenging to prepare for the exam given my ad-hoc travel schedules and long working hours. I was able to overcome the problem with some discipline and consistency and ensured that there were no 'cheat days' (when I could take a break from study). Additionally, overcoming this would not have been possible without the constant support of my wife, Sonila.

3. What are the 3 most important resources that helped your prepare for the exam?

a) PMBOK

b) Rita Mulcahy's PMP Exam Prep

c) The uncompromising 5-day tutorial program and the notes provided by my PMI REP instructor, Mr Sriprasad.

4. What are the 3 most useful strategies you employed to crack the PMP exam?

a) Ensure you don't read too many books - stick to two books, primarily.

b) Starting off with the PMBOK can be extremely dull and unnerving. Therefore, first try reading a book like Rita Mulcahy's PMP Exam Prep to put you at ease.

c) Understand how to solve the quantitative questions – it is a sure way to score well in the exam.

5. What would your most important advice to any PMP aspirant who wants to crack the exam on the first attempt be?

There is no shortcut to attending a good training program. It can make or break your PMP exam attempt. Attending the program only to gain the PDUs does not serve the intended purpose and I suggest allocating at least five continuous days for the training program and continuing the momentum by allocating 2 hours each day for about 45 days. This is a formula that worked well for me and should work well for PMP aspirants with busy schedules.

A FINAL NOTE

This book has been a summary of my experiences preparing for the PMP exam and is based on the methods and practices I adopted successfully. Nevertheless, it would be unwise to assume that one approach suits all.

The study calendar I provided has timeslots based on how I used my time, but it can be tweaked accordingly to suit your schedules. Just ensure that the number of hours you put in everyday remains more or less the same and that you dedicate enough time to cover the designated topic for the day.

I know many PMP professionals who used just one guide in addition to the PMBOK to prepare for the exam. In such cases, they did two passes (two iterations) of the same textbook. You can also follow that approach using the plan I have provided. But if you choose that road, make sure that you have a more thorough reading of the PMBOK also. If you are really short of funds and want to buy just one guide, I will suggest you to buy just Rita Mulcahy's

PEP in addition to the PMBOK. You will be getting the PMBOK for free when you register with the PMI (and there should be no reason that you don't register because the exam works out cheaper because of the subsidised exam fee for PMI members).

Lastly, passing the PMP is not that herculean a task. It is just something that needs some focussed effort and patience. If you follow the study approach I have outlined here judiciously, and practice simulation tests accordingly, you should do well.

All the best for the exam; may the force be with you!

Disclaimer: I have put in my best effort to give you accurate information on the methods and strategies that I pursued to attain a PMP certification in 30 days through this book. Nevertheless, this should not be interpreted as a promise or guarantee for your success. By the virtue of the guidance in this book, I am equipping you with those same tools that worked for me but any positive or negative outcome is ultimately dependent on your capability, commitment and effort.

YOUR FEEDBACK IS VALUABLE

Did you like this book and find it useful?

If yes, I would really appreciate it if you would let other readers know by posting a short review. Your review will help in giving me the much needed exposure in a crowded market place and help this book be discovered by others too!

You can post your review on the website from where you purchased this copy.

JOIN THE MONTHLY NEWSLETTER

There is a monthly newsletter dispatched to subscribers of **rojiabraham.com** that provides information about the author Roji's latest blog posts, books in focus by other featured authors and upcoming titles.

This monthly newsletter will also contain the occasional goodies like free downloads or discounts on featured titles!

To join the newsletter, go to the link provided below: **http://bitly.com/rojiabraham-newsletter**

Made in the USA
Middletown, DE
28 August 2017